Lesson Book 3 ▪

P i a n o

Willard A. Palmer ▪ Morton Manus ▪ Amanda Vick Lethco

Additional Pages: Andrew Higgins
Additional Artwork/Engraving: Oliver Wood
Additional Proofing: Leonie McCaughren
Cover Design: Holly Fraser

Produced by
Alfred Publishing Co. (UK) Ltd.
Burnt Mill, Elizabeth Way,
Harlow
Essex, CM20 2HX
alfreduk.com

© 2018 Alfred Publishing Co. (UK) Ltd.
All Rights Reserved. Printed in India.

ISBN-10: 1-4706-1308-5
ISBN-13: 978-1-4706-1308-2

Cover and Interior Illustrations by David Silverman (Painted by Cheryl Hennigar)

A Note From the Authors

Welcome to Alfred's Basic Graded Piano Course Book 3!

Congratulations on completing Alfed's Basic Graded Piano Course Book 2. Now you are ready to continue your journey and begin to prepare for your first exam. The Graded Course was written in response to many requests from teachers for an Alfred Course that will enable students to pass the graded exams that are so much a part of the learning experience throughout the world. It uses the Lesson book to introduce sight-reading and technique as well as preparation for pieces. It uses the correlated Theory book to prepare for the Theory exam at the same time. Book 3 moves toward the Grade 1 exam.

By including some exam pieces from previous practical syllabuses and also a mock theory paper from the theory exam in the correlated theory books, you, as a teacher, can judge perfectly the appropriate time to enter your pupil for the graded exam. This will make passing a formality but, more importantly, give your pupil the confidence to achieve the merits and distinctions that inspire and reward their hard work.

Here is a basic outline of the Grade 1 Lesson book:

pgs. 1-12	The Primary Triads and V7 chord in C and G
pgs. 13-20	Broken Chords; D Major Scale
pgs. 21-28	Extended Position; Major Scales in Contrary Motion
pgs. 29-34	F major; Chromatic Scale; Two Octave Scales
pgs. 35-46	Minor Keys; Triads and Scales in A and D
pgs. 47-52	Compound Time Signatures; Triplets
pgs. 53-65	Inversions; Broken Chords; Semi-quavers (sixteenth notes)

As you leaf through these books you will notice the clean and uncluttered page design and clear engraving, with attractive art work designed to complement the music and appeal to all.

The authors hope that these pages will help continue your journey into the WONDERFUL WORLD OF MUSIC.

Willard A. Palmer, Morton Manus & Amanda Vick Lethco

Triads

A **TRIAD** is a 3 note chord.

The three notes of a triad are:

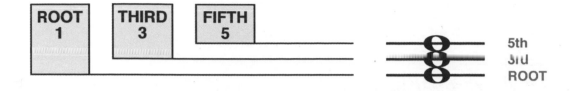

| ROOT 1 | THIRD 3 | FIFTH 5 |

5th
3rd
ROOT

The ROOT is the note from which the triad gets its name. The ROOT of a C triad is C.

Triads in ROOT POSITION (with the root at the bottom) always look like this:

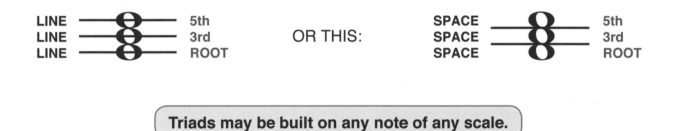

LINE — 5th
LINE — 3rd
LINE — ROOT

OR THIS:

SPACE — 5th
SPACE — 3rd
SPACE — ROOT

> **Triads may be built on any note of any scale.**

Triads in C

Play with RH:

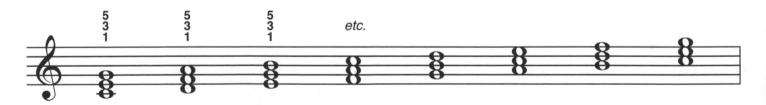

etc.

Play with LH:

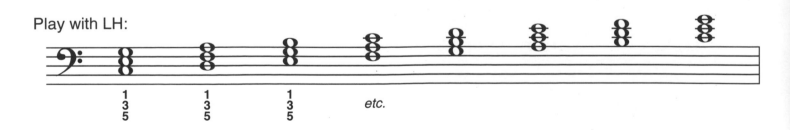

etc.

Triads in C

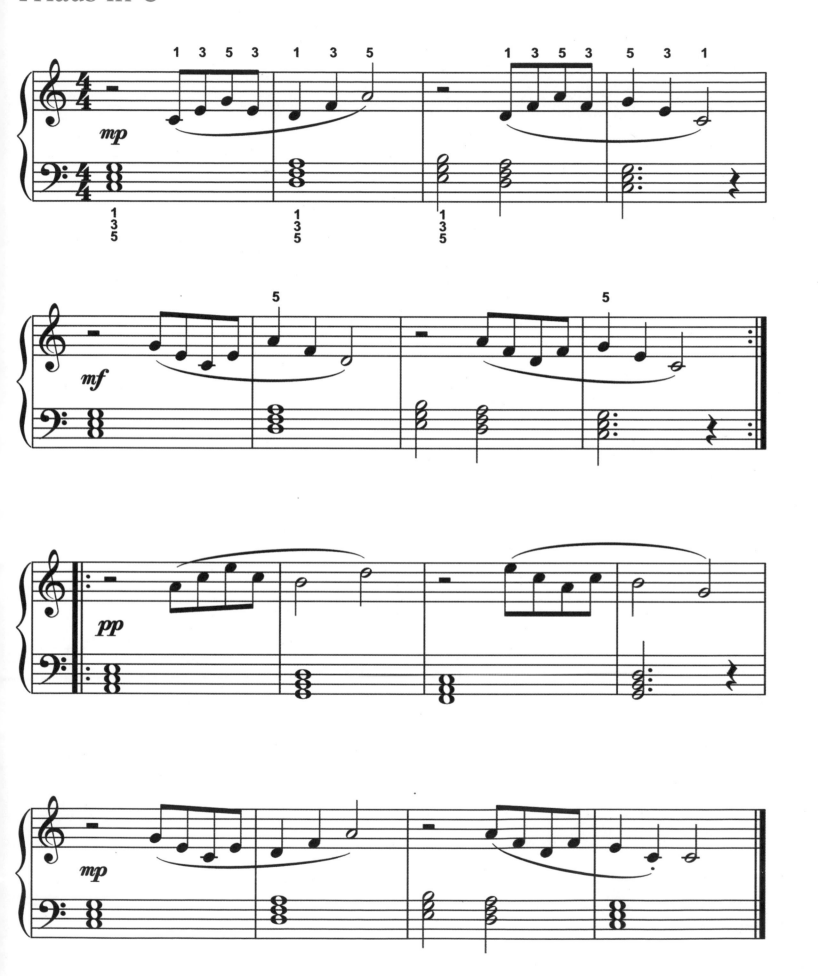

The Complete "Triad Vocabulary"

Play each of the following triads with LH 5 3 1, saying the names of the notes as you play, beginning with the lowest note of each triad.

Say: Play:

A C E

B D F

C E G

D F A

E G B

F A C

G B E

With this "vocabulary" you can play triads IN ANY KEY, simply by using the **KEY SIGNATURE**.

Memorise the complete "**Triad Vocabulary**".

Cockles and Mussels

Before you play this piece, say the names of the notes of each LH triad aloud. Begin with the LOWEST note of each triad.

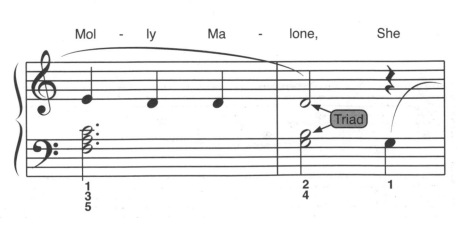

The "Triad Vocabulary" of this piece:

C E G   **D** F A   **E** G B   **F** A C   **G** B D

Important: Root position triads skip a letter between each note.

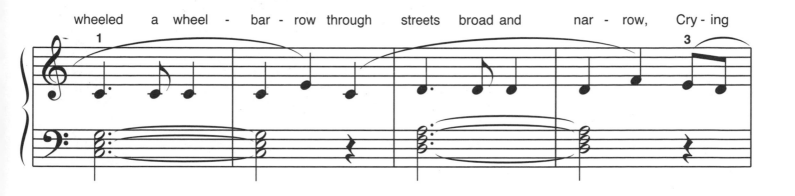

wheeled a wheel-bar-row through streets broad and nar-row, Cry-ing

Both hands
8va – – – –

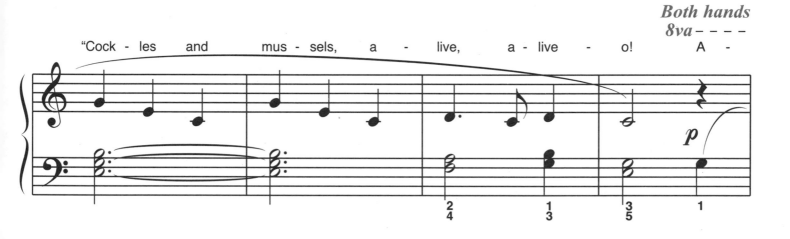

"Cock-les and mus-sels, a-live, a-live-o! A-

(Both hands 8va) – – – – – – – – – – – – –

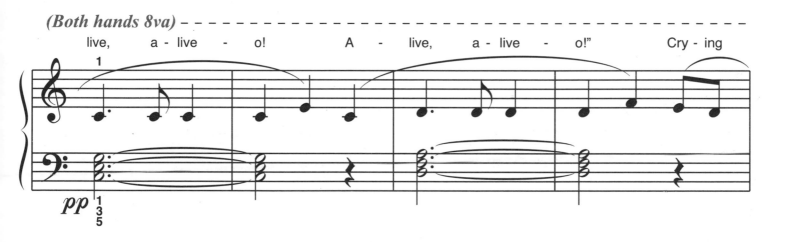

live, a-live-o! A-live, a-live-o!" Cry-ing

(Both hands 8va) – – – – – – – – – – – – –

"Cock-les and mus-sels, a-live, a-live-o!"

ritardando – – – – – – – – – – –

Square Dance

The Primary Triads

The three most important triads in any key are those built on the 1st, 4th, & 5th notes of the scale. These are called the **PRIMARY TRIADS** of the key.

The chords are identified by the Roman numerals, **I**, **IV**, & **V** (1, 4, & 5), and are called the **TONIC**, **SUBDOMINANT** and **DOMINANT** respectively.

In the key of C MAJOR, the **I CHORD** (1 chord) is the C TRIAD.
The **IV CHORD** (4 chord) is the F TRIAD.
The **V CHORD** (5 chord) is the G TRIAD.

The KEY SIGNATURE of the key of C MAJOR has no sharps or flats.

The Primary Triads in C Major

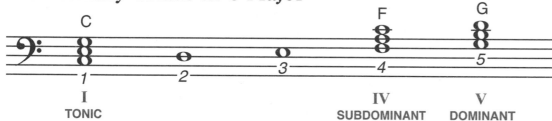

ROOT POSITION **I**, **IV** & **V** triads in C MAJOR. Play several times.

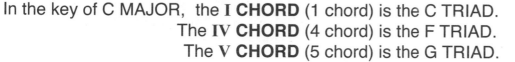

Chord Progressions

When we change from one chord to another, we call this a **CHORD PROGRESSION**.

When all chords are in root position, the hand must leap from one chord to the next when playing the primary triads.

To make the chord progressions easier to play and sound better, the **IV** and **V** chords may be played in other positions by moving one or more of the higher chord tones down an octave.

The **I** chord is played in ROOT POSITION: The top note of the **IV** chord is moved down an octave: The two top notes of the **V** chord are moved down an octave:

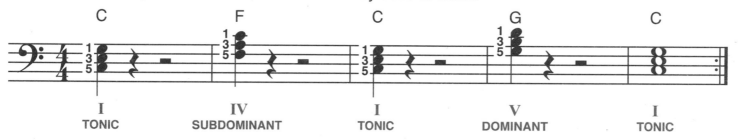

> When a triad is not in root position, the ROOT is ALWAYS the **upper** note of the interval of a 4th!

I, **IV**, & **V** triads in C MAJOR. Practise this line many times! Compare with the second line above!

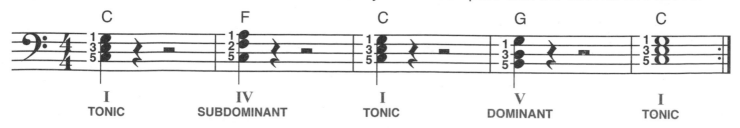

7

Got Those Blues!

Moderato

Play quavers in long-short pairs

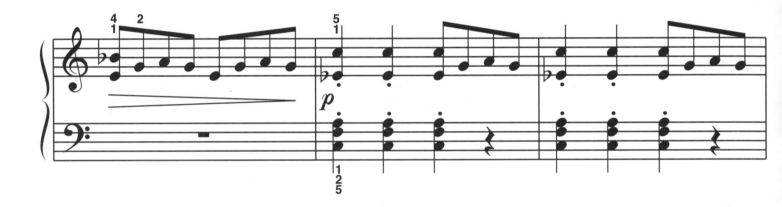

ritardando

The V 7 Chord

In many pieces a **V7 CHORD** is used instead of a **V TRIAD**.
To make a **V7** chord, a note an interval of a 7th above the root is added to the **V** triad:

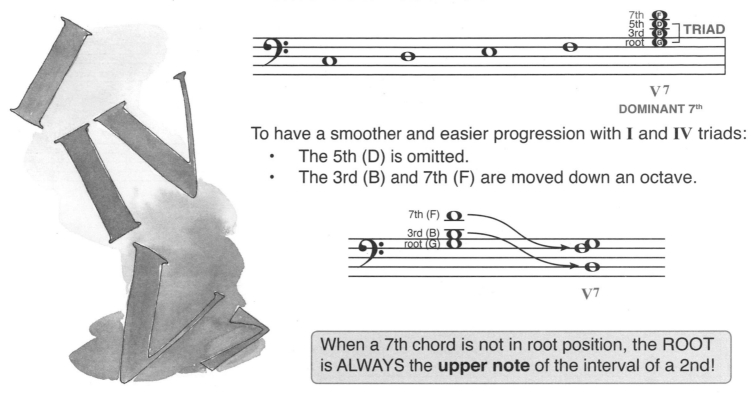

V7 built on the 5th note of the C MAJOR SCALE:

7th
5th
3rd
root
} TRIAD

V 7
DOMINANT 7th

To have a smoother and easier progression with **I** and **IV** triads:
- The 5th (D) is omitted.
- The 3rd (B) and 7th (F) are moved down an octave.

7th (F)
3rd (B)
root (G)

V7

When a 7th chord is not in root position, the ROOT is ALWAYS the **upper note** of the interval of a 2nd!

The Primary Chords in C Major

The three PRIMARY CHORDS are now **I**, **IV** & **V7**.

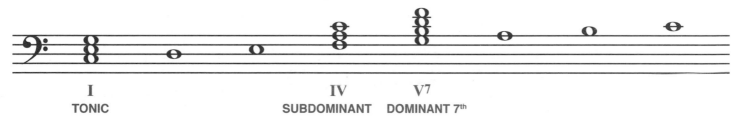

I
TONIC

IV
SUBDOMINANT

V7
DOMINANT 7th

The following positions are often used for smooth progressions:

C Major Chord Progression with I, IV & V7 Chords
Play several times each day!

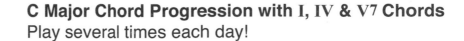

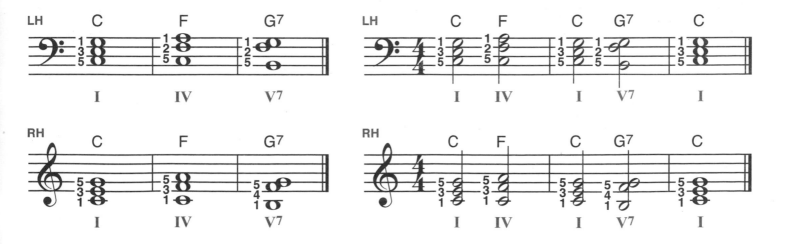

The Song That Never Ends!

Lightly swinging*

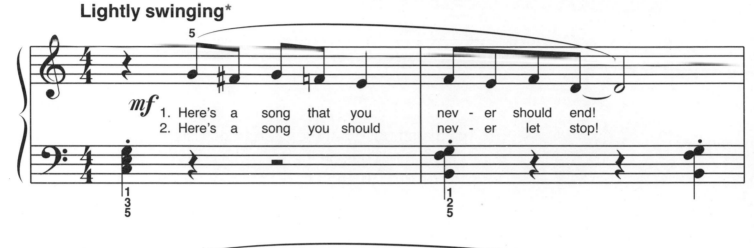

1. Here's a song that you nev - er should end!
2. Here's a song you should nev - er let stop!

Play it o - ver, then play it a - gain!
From the bot - tom, go back to the top!

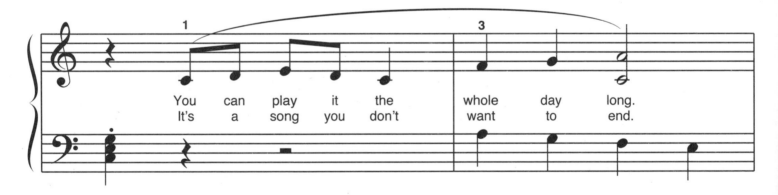

You can play it the whole day long.
It's a song you don't want to end.

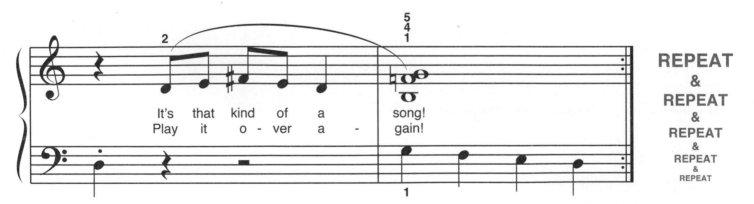

It's that kind of a song!
Play it o - ver a - gain!

REPEAT
&
REPEAT
&
REPEAT
&
REPEAT
&
REPEAT

*OPTIONAL: Quavers may be played in long-short pairs.

If you feel that you *must* end this song, don't stop at the last bar! Repeat the first four bars over and over, gradually fading away!

Got Lots-a Rhythm!

Moderate blues tempo*
2nd time RH 8va

*OPTIONAL: Quavers may be played in long-short pairs.

The Primary Chords in G Major

The KEY SIGNATURE of the KEY OF G MAJOR is ONE SHARP (F♯).

The 3 PRIMARY CHORDS in the key of G MAJOR are:

The **IV** and **V7** chords are moved to lower positions, for smooth and easy chord progressions:

Chord Progressions using I, IV & V7 Chords

Play with LH. Notice that the LH 5th finger plays the KEY-NOTE (G) on the **I** chord and the **IV** chord!

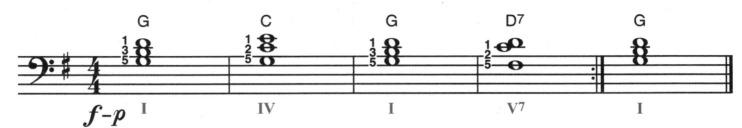

Play with RH. Notice that the RH thumb plays the KEY-NOTE (G) on the **I** chord and the **IV** chord!

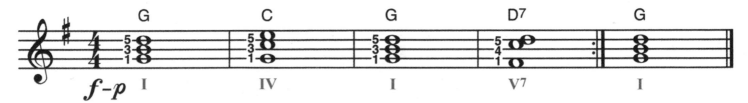

Play with both hands.

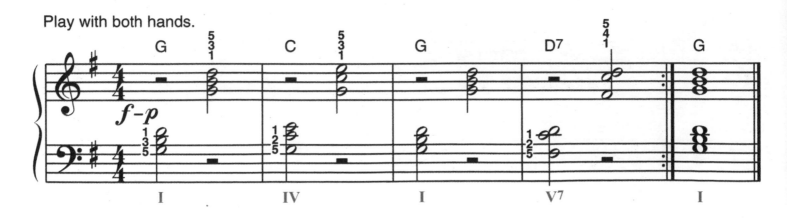

Why Am I Blue?

Moderately slow blues tempo*

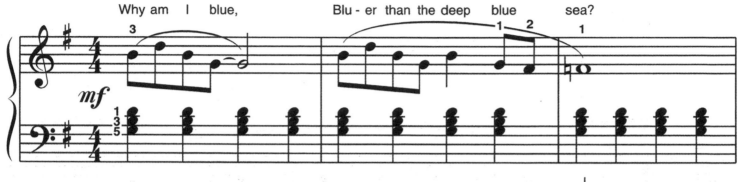

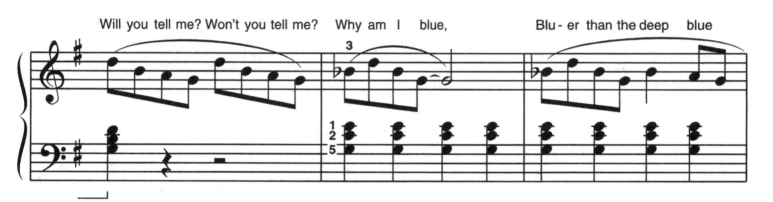

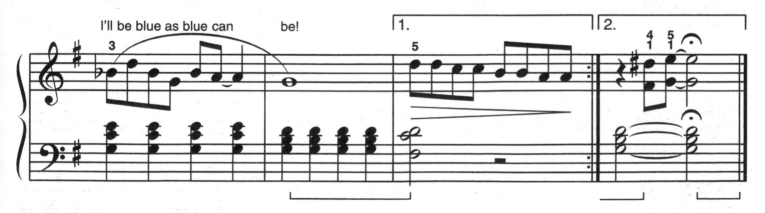

*OPTIONAL: Quavers may be played in long-short pairs.

Block Chords and Broken Chords

Chords are often used as follows:

1. BLOCK CHORDS (all notes together).

2. BROKEN CHORDS (one note at a time).

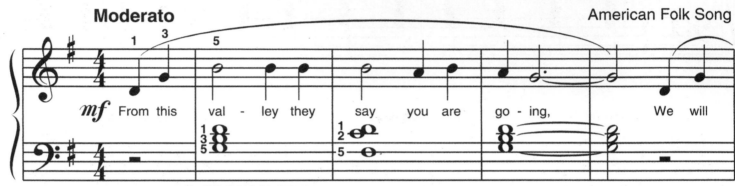

Red River Valley

RED RIVER VALLEY begins with the accompaniment played in BLOCK CHORDS. BROKEN CHORDS begin at the end of this page, and are used through the rest of the piece. Compare the two pages, bar by bar, before you play. The chords are the same.

Moderato

American Folk Song

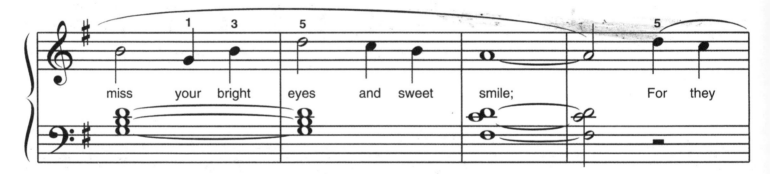

From this val - ley they say you are go - ing, We will

(BLOCK CHORD)

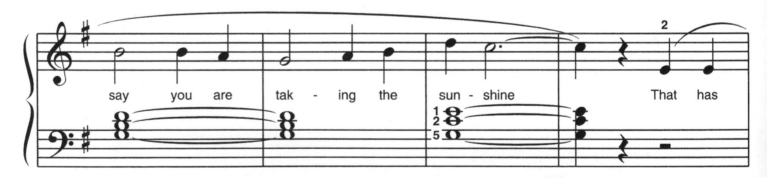

miss your bright eyes and sweet smile; For they

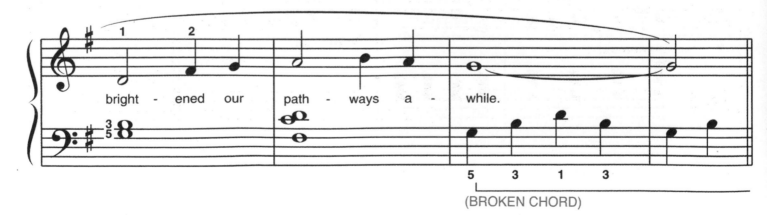

say you are tak - ing the sun - shine That has

bright - ened our path - ways a - while.

(BROKEN CHORD)

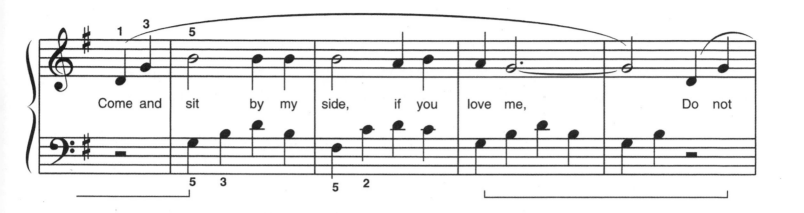

Come and sit by my side, if you love me, Do not

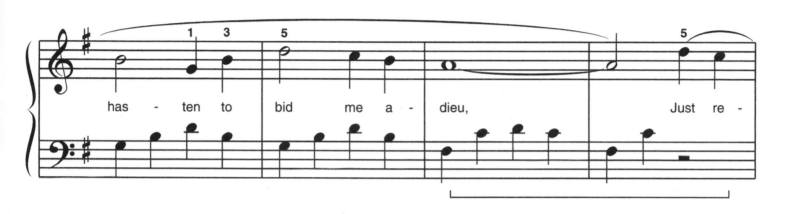

has - ten to bid me a - dieu, Just re -

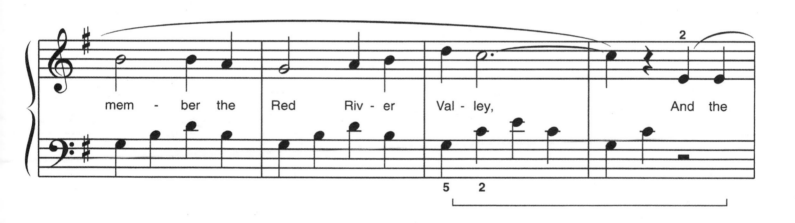

mem - ber the Red Riv - er Val - ley, And the

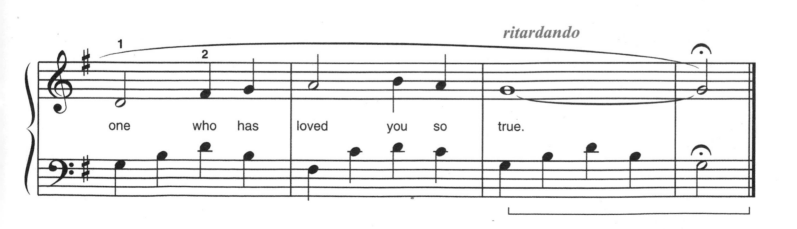

ritardando

one who has loved you so true.

D Major Scale

REMEMBER! The pattern of each tetrachord is: WHOLE TONE–WHOLE TONE–SEMITONE

1. Write the letter names of the notes of the D MAJOR SCALE, from left to right, on the keyboard below. Be sure the WHOLE TONES & SEMITONES are correct!

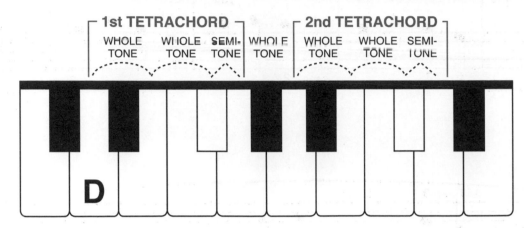

2. Complete the tetrachord beginning on D. Write one note over each finger number.

3. Complete the tetrachord beginning on A. Write one note over each finger number.

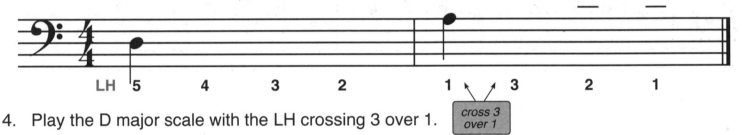

4. Play the D major scale with the LH crossing 3 over 1.

5. Write the finger numbers over the notes of the following scale, starting with 5 and crossing 3 over 1.

6. Play the D major scale with RH crossing 3 over 1.

D Major Scale in Contrary Motion

KEY OF D MAJOR
Key Signature: 2 sharps (F♯ & C♯)

Play hands separately at first, then together.
Begin slowly, gradually increasing speed.

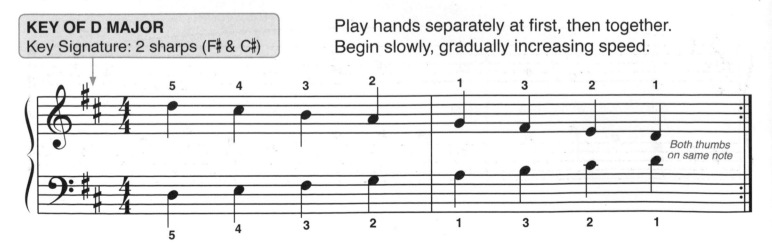

Calypso Carnival

KEY OF D MAJOR
Key Signature: 2 sharps (F♯ & C♯)

The Primary Chords in D Major

THE KEY SIGNATURE of the KEY OF D MAJOR has 2 SHARPS (F♯ & C♯).
The 3 PRIMARY CHORDS in the key of D MAJOR are:

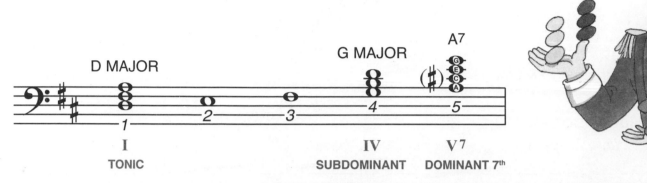

The **IV** and **V7** chords are moved to lower positions for smooth and easy chord progressions:

Chord Progressions using I, IV & V7 Chords

Play with LH.
Notice that the LH 5th finger plays the TONIC NOTE (D) on the **I** chord and the **IV** chord!

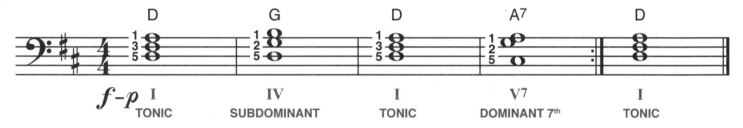

Play with RH.
Notice that the RH thumb plays the TONIC NOTE (D) on the **I** chord and the **IV** chord!

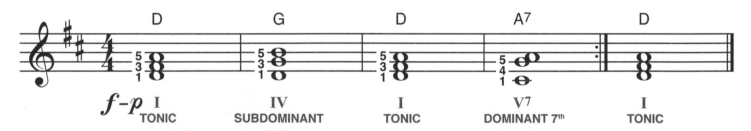

Play with both hands, then play as **broken chords**.

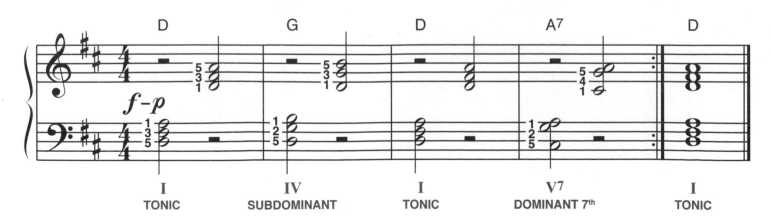

Oh! Susanna!

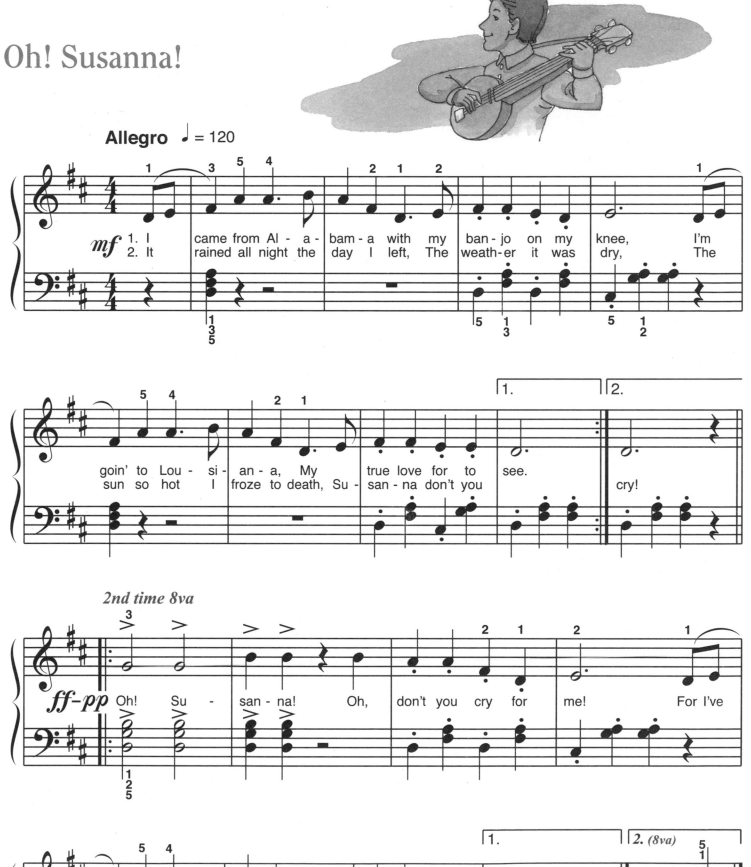

LH Warm-up

Practise many times, very slowly. These four bars contain everything new that you will find in the LH of *The Entertainer*!

The Entertainer

Not fast!*

Play quavers evenly

Scott Joplin
1868-1917

* "Not fast" is the composer's own indication.

RH: An Extended Position

ON TOP OF OLD SMOKY begins and ends
with the RH in an EXTENDED POSITION.

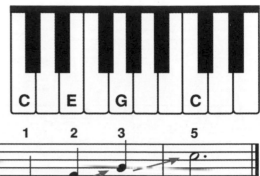

Play several times:

Up a 3rd   Up a 3rd   Up a 4th

LH Review: The Primary Chords in C

BLOCK CHORDS   **BROKEN CHORDS**

I   IV   V⁷   I   IV   V⁷

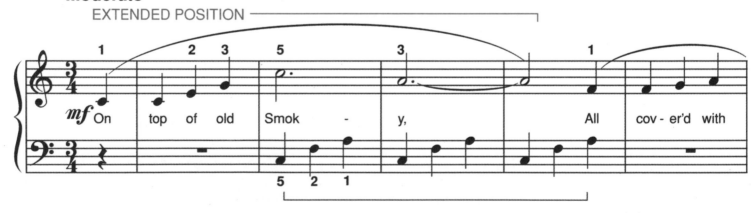

On Top of Old Smoky

Moderato

EXTENDED POSITION

mf On   top   of   old   Smok - y,   All   cov - er'd   with

snow,   I   lost   my   true   lov -

er, From a - court - in' too slow. For

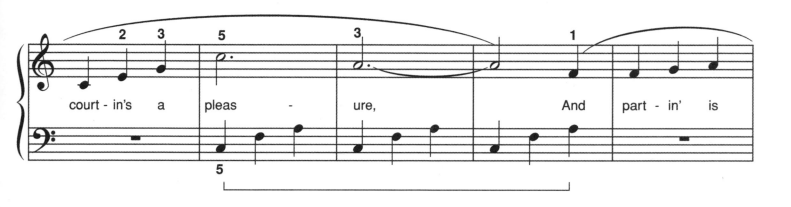

court - in's a pleas - ure, And part - in' is

grief, A false-heart-ed lov - er,

Is worse than a thief.

RH: More Extended Positions

FESTIVE MARCH contains two EXTENDED POSITIONS for the RH.

Play several times:

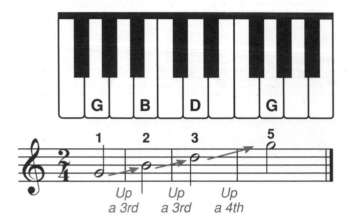

Play several times:

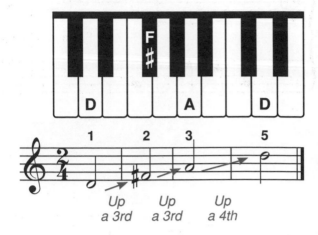

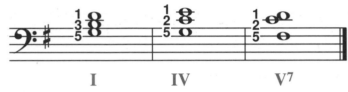

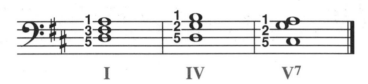

LH Review: The Primary Chords in D & G

THE KEY OF G

I   IV   V⁷

THE KEY OF D

I   IV   V⁷

Festive March

Joyfully

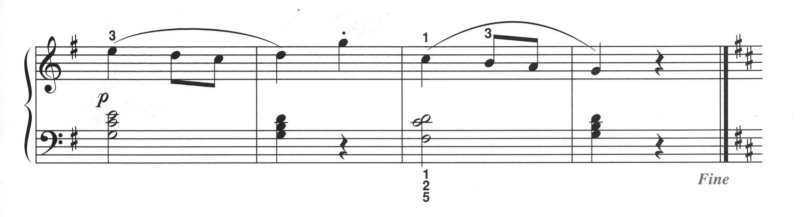

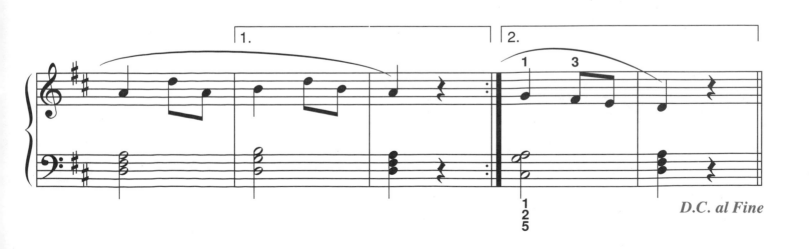

25

Review: Primary Chords with Both Hands

Alpine Melody

This piece uses ONLY the primary chords in C, G & D, in BOTH HANDS!

More About Major Scales in Contrary Motion

When the hands move in opposite directions, one ascending as the other descends, it is called CONTRARY MOTION.

Play hands separately, then together. Play slowly at first, then gradually increase speed.

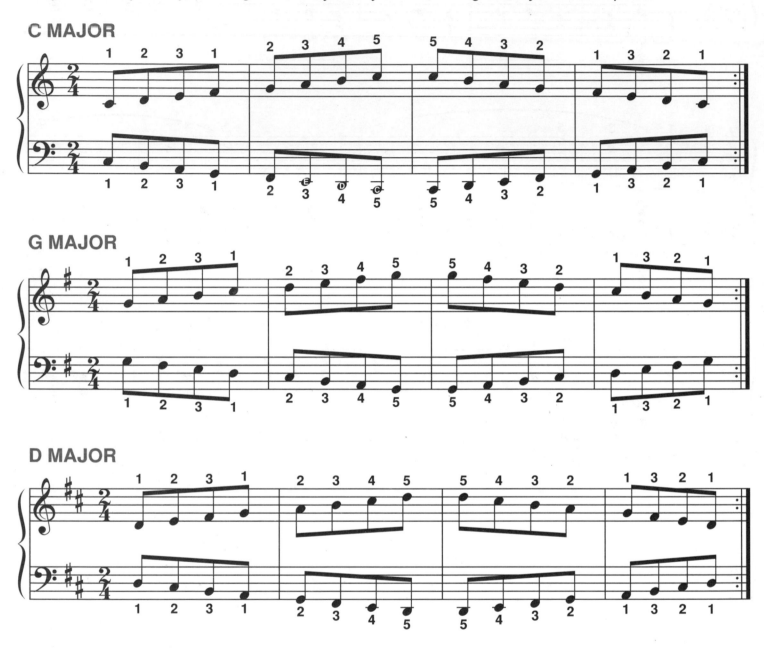

C MAJOR

G MAJOR

D MAJOR

Prelude in 18th Century Style

The F Major Scale

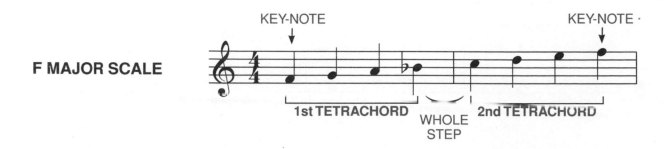

F MAJOR SCALE

The fingering for the F MAJOR SCALE with the LH is the same as for all the scales you have studied so far: 5 4 3 2 1 - 3 2 1 ascending; 1 2 3 - 1 2 3 4 5 descending.

Play slowly and carefully!

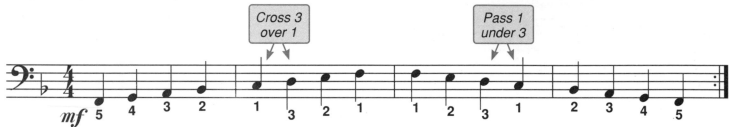

To play the F MAJOR SCALE with the RH, the 5th finger is not used! The fingers fall in the following groups: 1 2 3 4 - 1 2 3 4 ascending; 4 3 2 1 - 4 3 2 1 descending.

Play slowly and carefully!

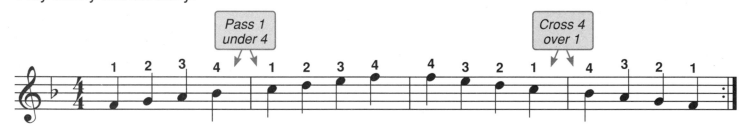

The F Major Scale in Contrary Motion

Play the hands separately at first, then together.
Begin slowly and gradually increase speed. Play several times daily.

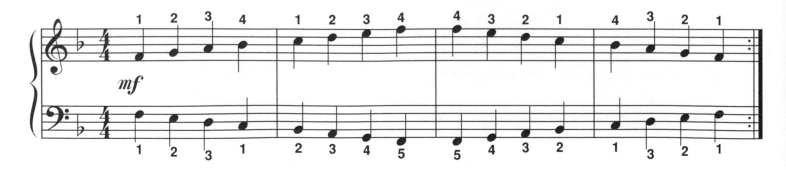

Casey Jones

KEY OF F MAJOR
Key signature: 1 flat (B♭)

Moderato

*Quavers may be played unevenly, in long-short pairs.

The Primary Chords in F Major

Reviewing the F MAJOR SCALE, LH ascending.

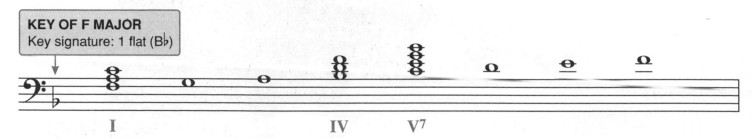

KEY OF F MAJOR
Key signature: 1 flat (B♭)

Primary Chords in F

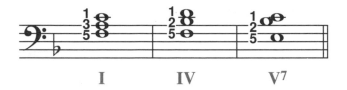

F Major Chord Progression
Play several times.

BLOCK CHORDS
Play.

BROKEN CHORDS
Play.

A Day in Vienna

Moderate waltz tempo

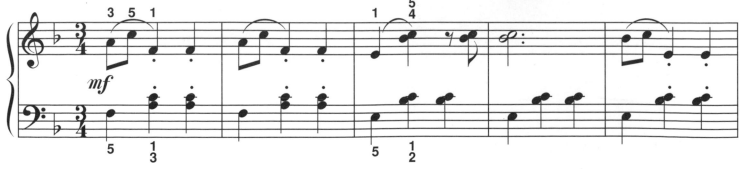

CHROMATIC SCALE

EXTENDED POSITION*

CHROMATIC SCALE

*EXTENDED POSITION: A white key is skipped between the 1st & 2nd fingers, and also between the 2nd & 3rd fingers. Two white keys are skipped between the 3rd & 5th fingers.

Major Scales

C Major Scale Parallel Motion One Octave

C Major Scale Two Octaves Hands Separately

Right Hand:

Left Hand:

G Major Scale Parallel Motion One Octave

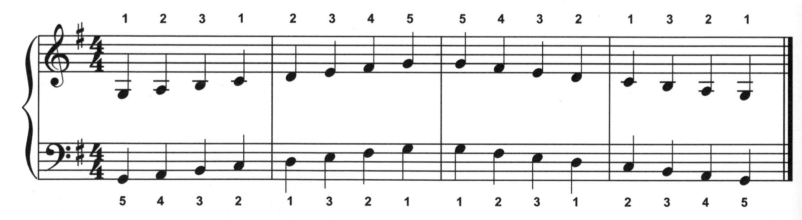

G Major Scale Two Octaves Hands Separately

Right Hand:

Left Hand:

D Major Scale Parallel Motion One Octave

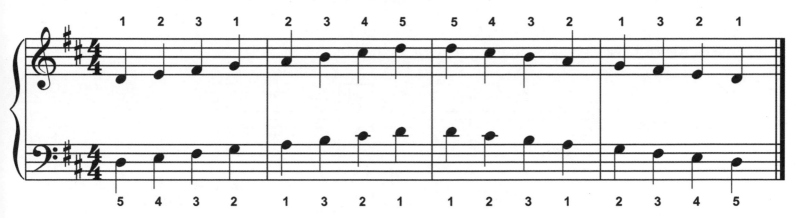

D Major Scale Two Octaves Hands Separately

Right Hand:

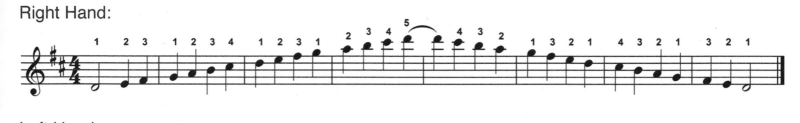

Left Hand:

F Major Scale Parallel Motion One Octave

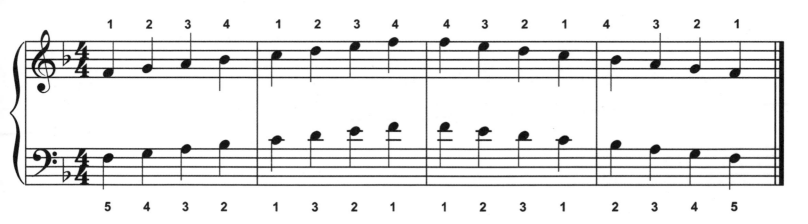

F Major Scale Two Octaves Hands Separately

Right Hand:

Left Hand:

Minor Scales

Every MAJOR KEY has a RELATIVE MINOR KEY that has the same KEY SIGNATURE.
The RELATIVE MINOR begins on the 6th TONE of the MAJOR SCALE.

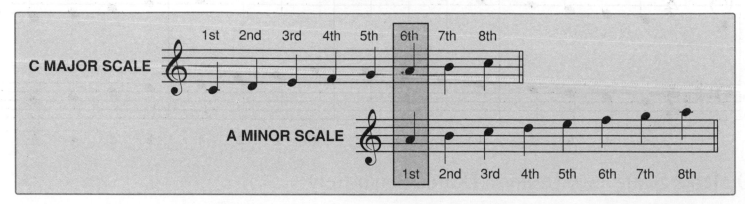

Because the keys of C MAJOR & A MINOR have the same KEY SIGNATURE
(no #'s, no ♭'s), they are RELATIVES.

The Key of A Minor (Relative of C Major)

There are *3 KINDS* of minor scales: the NATURAL, the HARMONIC, & the MELODIC.

Practise each of the following scales, first with the RH, as written,
then with the LH, 2 octaves lower than written.

1. THE NATURAL MINOR SCALE

This scale uses *only* the tones of the relative major scale.

2. THE HARMONIC MINOR SCALE

The 7th tone is raised one half step,
ASCENDING & DESCENDING.

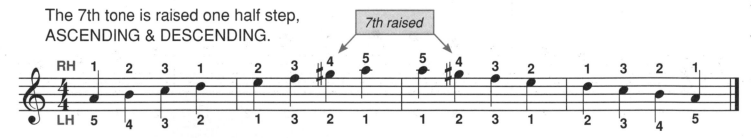

3. THE MELODIC MINOR SCALE

In the ASCENDING SCALE, the 6th (F) & 7th (G) tones are raised one half step.
The DESCENDING scale is the same as the natural minor.

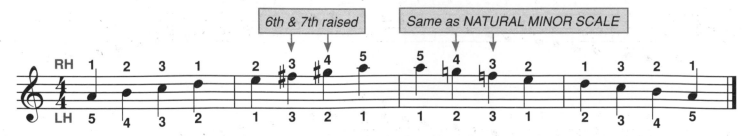

The HARMONIC minor is the most frequently used of the 3 minor scales.

The A Harmonic Minor Scale in Contrary Motion

Play several times daily!

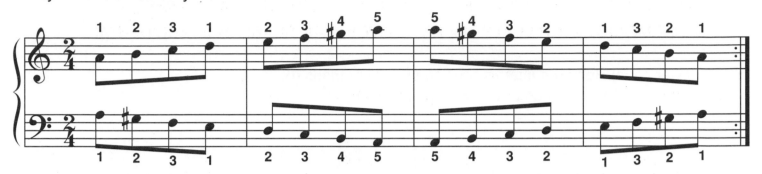

The A NATURAL MINOR and MELODIC MINOR SCALES may also be played in contrary motion by following the rules given on the preceding page.

Enchanted City

KEY OF A MINOR
Key signature: no #s, no ♭s

Andante moderato
2nd & 3rd time 8va

last time ritardando

Fine

loco (play as written, not 8va)

D.C. al Fine

The Primary Triads in Minor Keys

To find the primary triads in a MINOR KEY, the HARMONIC MINOR SCALE is used.

In the A HARMONIC MINOR SCALE, the 7th note (G) is made SHARP, as an ACCIDENTAL.

Small (lower case) Roman numerals are used for minor triads (i),
large (upper case) Roman numerals for major triads (V).

Notice that the **i** & **iv** chords are MINOR TRIADS. The **V** chord is a MAJOR TRIAD.
This is true in all minor keys!

To make the chord progressions easier to play and sound better,
the **iv** and **V** chords may be played in other positions by moving
one or more of the higher chord tones down an octave.

The **i** chord is
played in
ROOT POSITION:

The top note of the
iv chord is moved
down an octave:

The 2 top notes of the
V chord are moved
down an octave:

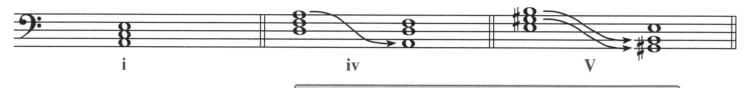

When a triad is not in root position, the ROOT is
ALWAYS the *upper note* of the interval of a 4th!

The Primary Triads in A Minor

Play several times.

These are the same chords, one octave higher
than the previous measures:

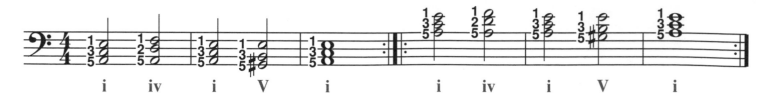

Go Down, Moses

Write the Roman numerals (**i**, **iv**, **V**) under the chords before you play.

KEY OF A MINOR
Key signature: no #s, no ♭s

Adagio moderato

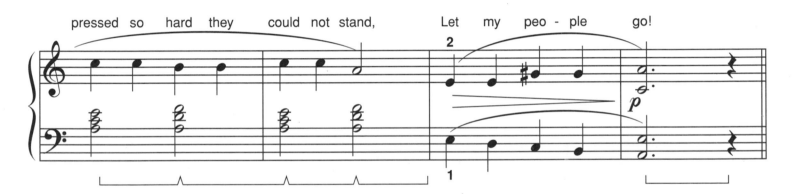

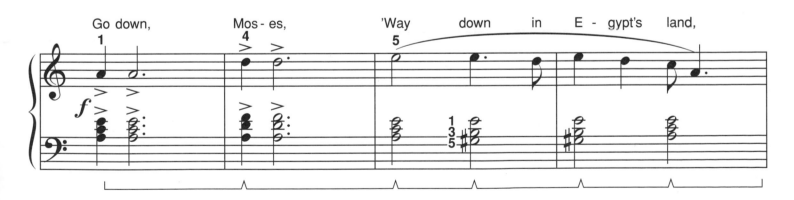

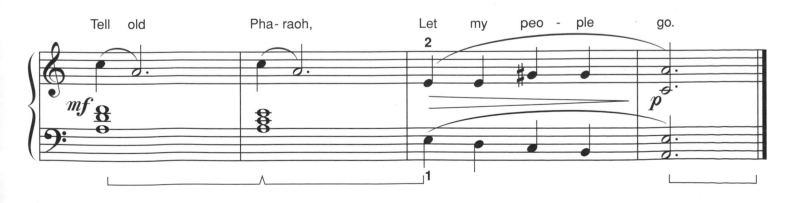

The Primary Chords in A Minor

USING V7 INSTEAD OF V

Remember: The **V7** chord is made by adding a 7th to the **V** triad.

V7

To play the chord so it makes a smoother progression, omit the 5th, and move the 3rd & 7th down an octave.

V7   V7

> When a 7th chord is not in root position, the ROOT is ALWAYS the *upper note* of the interval of a 2nd!

The 3 PRIMARY CHORDS are now **i**, **iv** & **V7**.   The same chords, one octave higher.

i   iv   V7   i   iv   V7
A MINOR   D MINOR   E7   A MINOR   D MINOR   E7

A MINOR PROGRESSION with broken **i**, **iv** & **V7** chords. Play several times.

5 3 1   5 2 1   5 3 1   5 2 1
i   iv   i   V7

> **KEY OF A MINOR**
> Key signature: no ♯s, no ♭s

Intermezzo*

Andante moderato

mf legato

5 3   5 2

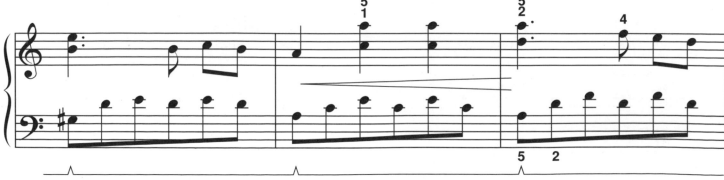

Intermezzo   Originally, music played between acts of an opera; now often used as the title of a short, independent piece.

KEY OF C MAJOR
(relative of A MINOR)

Allegro

2nd time both hands 8va

meno mosso*

D.C. al Fine

__Meno mosso__ means "less quickly." Play the last line considerably slower than the line before.

41

The Key of D Minor (Relative of F Major)

D MINOR is the relative of **F MAJOR.**

Both keys have the same key signature (1 flat, B♭).

REMEMBER: The RELATIVE MINOR begins on the 6th tone of the MAJOR SCALE.

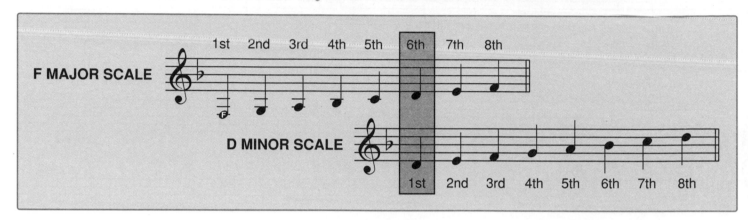

Practise each of the following scales, first with the RH, as written,
then with the LH, 2 octaves lower than written.

1. **THE NATURAL MINOR SCALE:** Use the same tones as the relative major scale.

2. **THE HARMONIC MINOR SCALE:** 7th (C) raised one half step, ASCENDING & DESCENDING.

3. **THE MELODIC MINOR SCALE:** 6th (B♭) & 7th (C) raised one half step (to B♮ & C♯) ASCENDING; descends like natural minor.

The D Harmonic Minor Scale in Contrary Motion

Play several times daily!

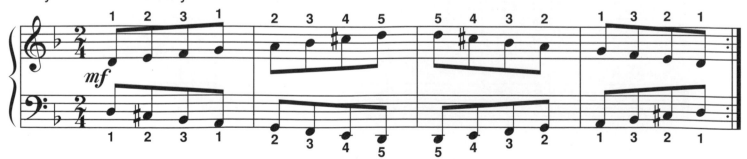

The D NATURAL MINOR and MELODIC MINOR scales may also be played in contrary motion.

Scarborough Fair

KEY OF D MINOR
Key signature: 1 flat (B♭)

Andante moderato

2nd time 8va

Are you goin' to Scar - bor-ough fair? Pars-ley, sage, rose - mar-y and thyme. Re -

mem - ber me to one who lives there. She was

once a true love of mine.

The Primary Chords in D Minor

Reviewing the D MINOR SCALE, LH ascending.

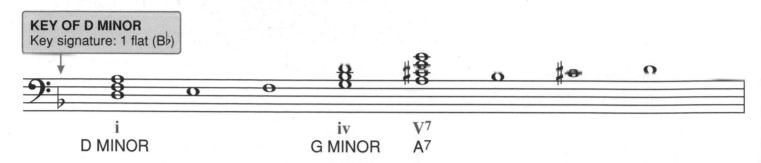

KEY OF D MINOR
Key signature: 1 flat (B♭)

i   iv   V⁷

D MINOR   G MINOR   A⁷

The following positions are often used for smooth progressions:

i   iv   V⁷

D MINOR   G MINOR   A⁷

D Minor Chord Progression. Play several times.

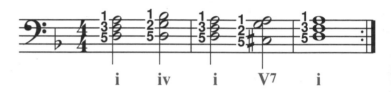

i   iv   i   V⁷   i

D MINOR PROGRESSION with broken **i**, **iv** & **V⁷** chords. Play several times.

Raisins and Almonds

Allegro moderato

mf When   I   was   a   ti - ny sleep-y - head,   Ma - ma

mp

Minor Scales

A Minor Scale Parallel Motion One Octave

A Minor Scale Two Octaves Hands Separately

Right Hand:

Left Hand:

D Minor Scale Parallel Motion One Octave

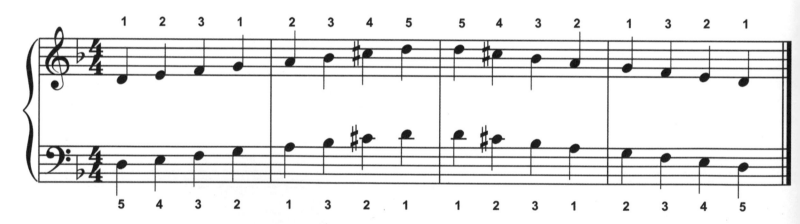

D Minor Scale Two Octaves Hands Separately

Right Hand:

Left Hand:

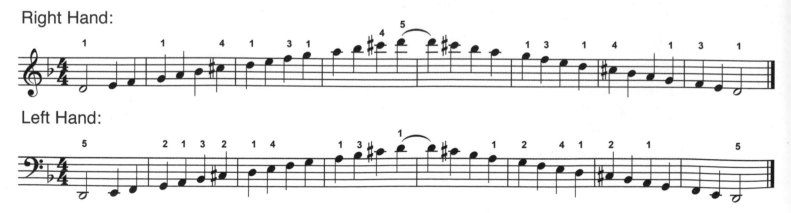

Sight-Reading in Minor Keys

A New Time Signature

3/8 means **3** beats in each bar.

3/8 a **quaver** gets one beat.

Clap (or tap) the following rhythms.
Clap **ONCE** for each note, counting aloud.

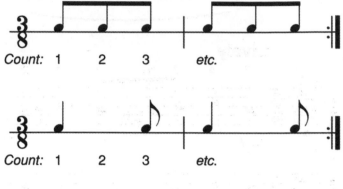

♪ = QUAVER (or **𝄾** REST)
Count "1"

♩ = CROTCHET (or **𝄽** REST)
Count "1-2"

♩. = DOTTED CROTCHET
Count "1-2-3"
For a WHOLE bar of silence,
a **▬** SEMIBREVE (WHOLE) REST is used

Count: 1   2   3   *etc.*

Hunting Song

Allegro moderato

*Tan - ti - vy, tan - ti - vy, tan - ti - vy,   A - hunt - ing

*A hunting call, imitating the sound of a horn.

A New Time Signature

6/8 means 6 beats in each bar.
a **quaver** gets one beat.

Clap (or tap) the following rhythms.
Clap **ONCE** for each note, counting aloud.

♪ = QUAVER (or ⅞ REST)
Count "1"

Count: 1 2 3 4 5 6 *etc.*

♩ = CROTCHET (or 𝄽 REST)
Count "1-2"

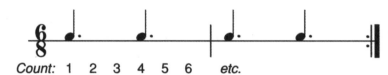

Count: 1 2 3 4 5 6 *etc.*

♩. = DOTTED CROTCHET
(or 𝄽 ⅞ RESTS)
Count "1-2-3"

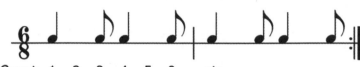

Count: 1 2 3 4 5 6 *etc.*

♩. = DOTTED MINIM
Count "1-2-3-4-5-6"
For a WHOLE bar of silence,
a ▬ SEMIBREVE REST is used.

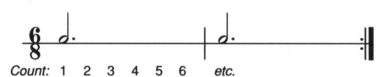

Count: 1 2 3 4 5 6 *etc.*

La Raspa
A Mexican Stamping Dance

Allegro
*2nd time accelerando poco a poco al fine**

mf

* *Accelerando* means "gradually faster." *Poco a poco* means "little by little."
Accelerando poco a poco al fine means "gradually faster little by little to the end."

1. *To next strain* 2. *(Fine)*

Fine

D.C. al Fine

*𝒔𝒇 or 𝒔𝒇𝒛 = *sforzando,* Italian for "forcing." It means to play louder on one note
or chord; in this case, it applies to the note above 𝒔𝒇 and the chord below it.

Quaver Triplets

When three notes are grouped together with a figure *3* above or below the notes, the group is called a **TRIPLET.**

The THREE NOTES of a
          QUAVER TRIPLET GROUP = ONE CROTCHET

When a piece contrains triplets, count "TRIP-A-LET"
                         or "ONE & THEN"
                         or any way suggested by your teacher.

Practise these warm-ups before playing the next piece.

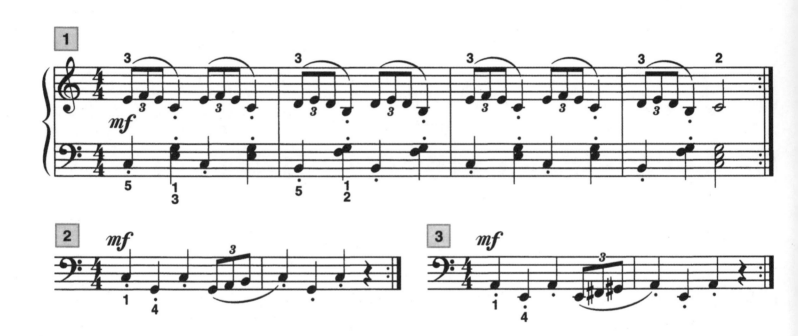

1. How many quaver triplets could you fit into one bar of the following time signatures?

$\frac{3}{4}$ = ☐ $\frac{2}{4}$ = ☐ $\frac{4}{4}$ = ☐

The Echo

Theodor Oesten
(1813-70)

Pastorale ♩ = 96

53

Triads: The 1st Inversion

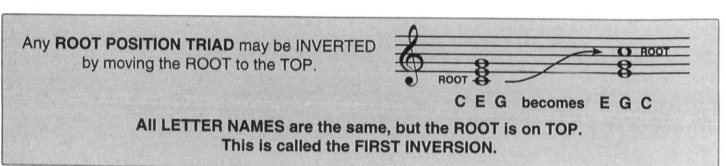

Any **ROOT POSITION TRIAD** may be INVERTED by moving the ROOT to the TOP.

C E G becomes E G C

All **LETTER NAMES** are the same, but the ROOT is on TOP.
This is called the **FIRST INVERSION**.

1st Inversion Triads in C

Play with RH. Use 1 2 5 on each triad.

Play the above with LH ONE OCTAVE LOWER. Use 5 3 1 on each triad.

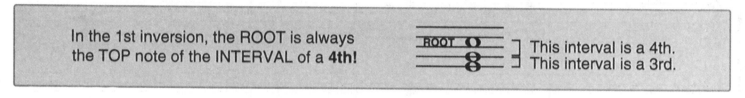

In the 1st inversion, the ROOT is always the TOP note of the INTERVAL of a **4th**!

This interval is a 4th.
This interval is a 3rd.

Draw an arrow to the ROOT of each of the following triads.

If there is an interval of a 4th in the triad, the TOP note of the 4th is the ROOT.
If there is no 4th, the LOWEST note is the ROOT.

Play with RH.

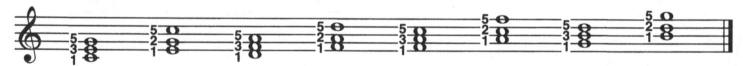

The Hokey-Cokey

Slow rock tempo

Traditional

All of the chords in this piece are 1st inversion triads except three.
Find those three and name them before you play.

LH staccato

ARPEGGIATED CHORDS

When a wavy line appears beside a chord, the chord is *arpeggiated* (broken or rolled). Play the lowest note first, and quickly add the next higher notes one at a time until the chord is complete. The first note is played on the beat.

Prelude in A Minor

Andante moderato

Both hands
8va 2nd time -

loco (as written) both times

ritardando

2nd time
both hands
8va segue

a tempo

*simile**

* *Simile* means *in the same manner*. In this case, continue playing triplets even though the **3**'s do not appear over or under the three-note groups.

Morendo means "dying away."

Triads: The 2nd Inversion

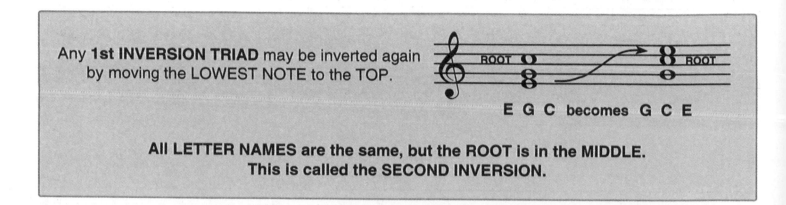

Any **1st INVERSION TRIAD** may be inverted again by moving the LOWEST NOTE to the TOP.

E G C becomes G C E

**All LETTER NAMES are the same, but the ROOT is in the MIDDLE.
This is called the SECOND INVERSION.**

2nd Inversion Triads in C

Play with LH. Use 5 2 1 on each triad.

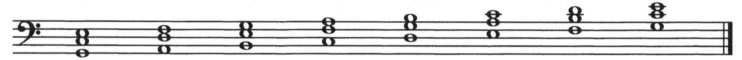

Play the above with RH ONE OCTAVE HIGHER. Use 1 3 5 on each triad.

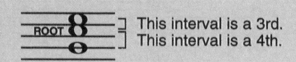

In the 2nd inversion, the ROOT is always the TOP note of the INTERVAL of a **4th!**

This interval is a 3rd.
This interval is a 4th.

Draw an arrow to the ROOT of each of the following triads.
   If there is an interval of a 4th in the triad, the TOP note of the 4th is the ROOT.
   If there is no 4th, the LOWEST note is the ROOT.

Play with RH.

REMEMBER: If the root is on the *bottom*, the triad is in **ROOT POSITION.**
If the root is on the *top*, the triad is in the **1st INVERSION.**
If the root is in the *middle*, the triad is in the **2nd INVERSION.**

Play the last line of music above with the RH, saying:

"ROOT POSITION, 1st INVERSION, 2nd INVERSION," etc., as you play.

Space Shuttle Blues

Play the LH alone first, naming the root of each triad.
Every LH chord is a 2nd inversion triad, so the root is always the MIDDLE note!

*Play the pairs of quavers slightly unevenly, long-short.
**Notice that the time signature changes for one bar only.

Triads in All Positions

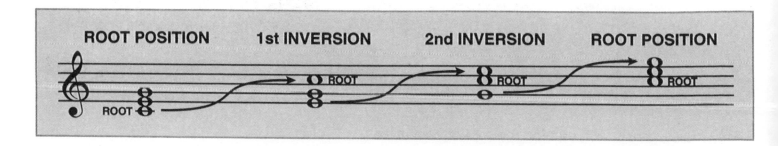

Play the following:

C Major Triad

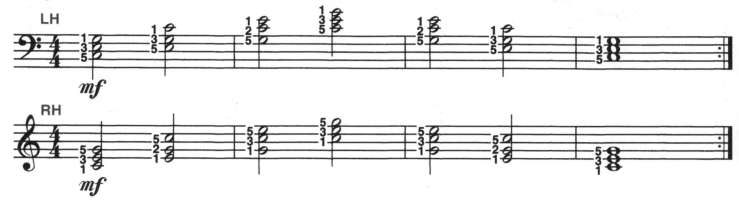

G Major Triad

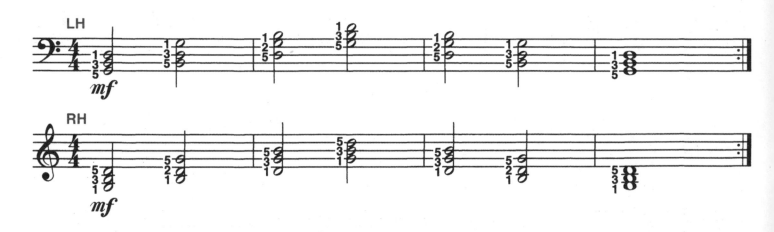

The same, beginning one octave higher:

IMPORTANT! Repeat all of the above,
using ARPEGGIATED CHORDS:

etc.

Farewell to Thee (Aloha Oe)

"Aloha OE" is used in the Hawaiian Islands as a greeting or farewell. This well-known song, which is played and sung for tourists arriving and leaving the Islands, was composed by the last queen of the Hawaiian Islands, Lydia Kamekaha Liliokalani, who reigned between 1891 and 1893.

Queen L. K. Liliuokalani

Adagio

2nd time play both hands 8va throughout

Broken Chord Etude

Moderato

Broken Chord Etude II

63

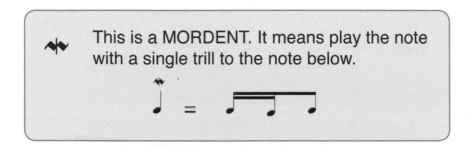

This is a MORDENT. It means play the note with a single trill to the note below.

Giga

Arnold
(1740-1802)

Moderato ♩. = 80-86

Semiquavers

When one semiquaver is written alone, it looks like this:

Semiquavers are usually in **pairs** or **groups of four**, written like this: ♪ **OR** ♪

Four semiquavers are played in the time of **one crotchet.**

COUNT: 1 - a - & - a

There can be 16 semiquavers in one bar of COMMON ($\frac{4}{4}$) TIME!

♪ = Semiquaver rest

Play several times: first ADAGIO, then ANDANTE, then ALLEGRO MODERATO.

CHALLENGE: Rewrite the above exercise on the stave below, replacing ONE SEMIQUAVER in each group of four with ONE SEMIQUAVER REST.

Grace Notes

A grace note is a type of musical ornament, usually printed smaller than regular notes. The SHORT GRACE NOTE, or ACCIACATURA (crushed note), appears as a small note with a stroke through the stem and is played at the same time as the main note. The LONG GRACE NOTE, or APPOGGIATURA, has not stroke and is played before the main note.

The Ballet

Daniel G. Turk
(1750-1813)

Certificate of Promotion

This is to certify that

_____

has successfully completed

Alfred's Basic Graded Piano Course Book 3

_____   _____
Date   Teacher